Always be
YOURSELF
unless you can be a
UNICORN

Racehorse Publishing

To: ....

From: ....

Shine BRIGHT ✦ like a ✦ UNICORN.

WHEN YOU KNOW YOURSELF, YOU ARE EMPOWERED. WHEN YOU ACCEPT YOURSELF, YOU ARE INVINCIBLE.

TINA LIFFORD

DON'T WASTE YOUR
ENERGY TRYING TO
CHANGE OPINIONS . . .
DO YOUR THING,
AND DON'T CARE IF
THEY LIKE IT.

LIVE YOUR LIFE IN FULL

color

WITH A SPRINKLING OF

glitter.

IT IS
CONFIDENCE
IN OUR BODIES,
MINDS, AND SPIRITS
THAT ALLOWS US
TO KEEP LOOKING
FOR NEW
ADVENTURES.

OPRAH WINFREY

YOU HAVE
TO BELIEVE IN
YOURSELF WHEN
NO ONE ELSE WILL.

SARAH MICHELLE GELLAR

NEVER DULL YOUR SHINE FOR ANYBODY ELSE.

TYRA BANKS

THE MOST COURAGEOUS ACT IS STILL TO THINK FOR YOURSELF. ALOUD.

COCO CHANEL

spirit

animal:

unicorn

Trust yourself;
BELIEVE
✦ **that you have a** ✦
UNIQUE DESTINY
to fulfill.

Candy Paull

WHEN SOMEONE
TOLD ME I LIVED IN A
FANTASY WORLD,
I ALMOST FELL OFF
MY UNICORN.

I DON'T LIKE TO GAMBLE, BUT IF THERE'S ONE THING I'M WILLING TO BET ON, IT'S MYSELF.

BEYONCÉ

ALWAYS BE A FIRST-RATE VERSION OF YOURSELF AND NOT A SECOND-RATE VERSION OF SOMEONE ELSE.

JUDY GARLAND

FOLLOW

your

OWN

star.

DANTE ALIGHIERI

LIVE,

LAUGH,

Sparkle.

THERE IS NO INTELLECTUAL OR EMOTIONAL SUBSTITUTE FOR THE AUTHENTIC, THE ORIGINAL, THE UNIQUE MASTERPIECE.

PAUL MELLON

ANYTHING IS POSSIBLE
ONCE YOU BELIEVE
YOU ARE WORTHY
OF ACHIEVING IT.

JASON POCKRANDT

Be a UNICORN

in a world of

HORSES

Nothing
can dim
the light
that shines
from within.

MAYA ANGELOU

WHEN YOU DISCOVER
SOMETHING THAT
NOURISHES YOUR SOUL,
CARE ENOUGH ABOUT
YOURSELF TO MAKE ROOM
FOR IT IN YOUR LIFE.

JEAN SHINODA BOLEN

ONCE YOU CHOOSE HOPE, ANYTHING IS POSSIBLE.

CHRISTOPHER REEVE

BORN

WILD

AND

FREE

THE DREAMERS ARE THE SAVIORS OF THE WORLD.

JAMES ALLEN

DON'T LET

them

TAME

you.

ALWAYS
BELIEVE AND
THERE WILL
ALWAYS BE
MAGIC.

CHERISH
FOREVER WHAT
MAKES YOU UNIQUE,
'CUZ YOU'RE REALLY
A YAWN IF IT GOES.

BETTE MIDLER

JUST BE YOURSELF. THERE IS NO ONE BETTER.

TAYLOR SWIFT

Unfold
your own
MYTH.

Rumi

Your
sparkle
brings light
To The
world.

WE HAVE TO
DARE TO BE
OURSELVES,
HOWEVER
FRIGHTENING
OR STRANGE
THAT SELF MAY
PROVE TO BE.

MAY SARTON

ALWAYS ACT LIKE YOU'RE WEARING AN INVISIBLE CROWN.

ANONYMOUS

BE FOREVER

magical.

MOST OF THE SHADOWS OF THIS LIFE ARE CAUSED BY STANDING IN ONE'S OWN SUNSHINE.

RALPH WALDO EMERSON

Always be

YOURSELF . . .

do not go out and look for a

SUCCESSFUL PERSONALITY

and try to

duplicate it.

Bruce Lee

KISSES ARE A BETTER

fate

THAN

wisdom.

E. E. CUMMINGS

RELEASE YOUR INNER UNICORN.

BEAUTY IS WHEN
YOU CAN APPRECIATE
YOURSELF. WHEN YOU
LOVE YOURSELF, THAT'S
WHEN YOU'RE MOST
BEAUTIFUL.

ZOË KRAVITZ

TALK TO YOURSELF LIKE YOU WOULD TO SOMEONE YOU LOVE.

BRENÉ BROWN

DARE TO BE DIFFERENT AND TO SET YOUR OWN PATTERN, LIVE YOUR OWN LIFE, AND FOLLOW YOUR OWN STAR.

WILFERD PETERSON

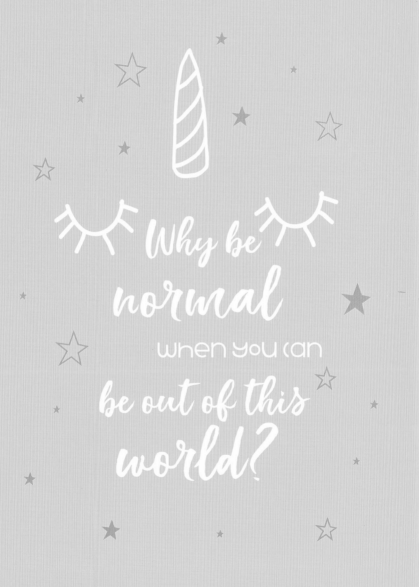

Why be
normal
when you can
be out of this
world?

BE YOURSELF.

THE WORLD WORSHIPS

THE ORIGINAL.

INGRID BERGMAN

I DO NOT
CARE SO MUCH
WHAT I AM TO
OTHERS AS I
CARE WHAT I AM
TO MYSELF.

MICHEL DE MONTAIGNE

LEAVE A LITTLE SPARKLE WHEREVER YOU GO.

OPTIMISM

is the faith that leads to

ACHIEVEMENT.

Nothing can be done without

HOPE AND CONFIDENCE.

Helen Keller

YOU ARE

magnificent

BEYOND MEASURE,

perfect

IN YOUR IMPERFECTIONS, AND

wonderfully made.

ABIOLA ABRAMS

A UNICORN TROTS TO THE BEAT OF ITS OWN DRUM.

IF YOU'RE PRESENTING YOURSELF WITH CONFIDENCE, YOU CAN PULL OFF PRETTY MUCH ANYTHING.

KATY PERRY

YOU'RE AWAKE, YOU'RE AWESOME. LIVE LIKE IT.

ROBBY NOVAK

DO NOT DOUBT THE

goodness

IN YOU.

DODINSKY

Some days I sit on the sofa and eat cake. Other days I UNICORN.

IF YOU ARE GOING TO DOUBT SOMETHING, DOUBT YOUR LIMITS.

DON WARD

You need to

BELIEVE

in yourself and what you do.

Be

TENACIOUS AND GENUINE.

Christian Louboutin

LET YOUR SPARKLE CHANGE THE WORLD, BUT DON'T LET THE WORLD CHANGE YOUR SPARKLE.

NEVER GIVE UP ON A
DREAM JUST BECAUSE OF
THE TIME IT WILL TAKE TO
ACCOMPLISH IT. THE TIME
WILL PASS ANYWAY.

EARL NIGHTINGALE

FOLLOW YOUR INNER

moonlight;

DON'T HIDE THE

madness.

ALLEN GINSBERG

THE GREATEST DOER MUST ALSO BE THE GREATEST DREAMER.

THEODORE ROOSEVELT

INHALE
JOY;
EXHALE
GLITTER.

LOVE YOURSELF
FIRST AND
EVERYTHING ELSE
FALLS INTO LINE.

LUCILLE BALL

EXPAND YOUR DREAMS . . . DARE TO TAP INTO YOUR GREATNESS.

ROBIN SHARMA

A

spoonful of

unicorn

makes life

more fun.

DREAMS ARE FREE, SO FREE YOUR DREAMS.

ANONYMOUS

It ain't what they
CALL YOU;
it's what you
ANSWER TO.

W. C. Fields

ALIVE
WHO'S YOUER
THAN
YOU!

DR. SEUSS

WORK HARD TODAY; SHINE BRIGHTER TOMORROW.

OUR
aspirations
ARE OUR
possibilities.

SAMUEL JOHNSON

CAPTURE YOUR DREAMS AND YOUR LIFE BECOMES FULL. YOU CAN, BECAUSE YOU THINK YOU CAN.

NIKITA KOLOFF

WALK WITH A

swish

IN YOUR TAIL AND

sass

IN YOUR STEP.

DIFFERENT IS
GOOD. SO DON'T FIT IN,
DON'T SIT STILL, DON'T
EVER TRY TO BE LESS
THAN WHAT YOU ARE.

ANGELINA JOLIE

To accomplish GREAT THINGS, we must not only act, but also DREAM; not only plan, but also believe.

Anatole France

Stay
focused
and
sparkly.

IF MY MIND CAN CONCEIVE IT, IF MY HEART CAN BELIEVE IT, I KNOW I CAN ACHIEVE IT!

JESSE JACKSON

DREAMS ARE
ILLUSTRATIONS . . . FROM
THE BOOK YOUR SOUL IS
WRITING ABOUT YOU.

MARSHA NORMAN

WHATEVER YOU DO, OR DREAM YOU CAN, BEGIN IT. BOLDNESS HAS GENIUS AND POWER AND MAGIC IN IT.

JOHN ANSTER

WHY WISH UPON A SHOOTING STAR WHEN YOU CAN RIDE ON ONE?

DO NOT BE EMBARRASSED BY YOUR

failures,

LEARN FROM THEM AND

start again.

RICHARD BRANSON

DREAMS ARE THE TOUCHSTONES OF OUR CHARACTERS.

HENRY DAVID THOREAU

BE
UNAPOLOGETICALLY
YOU.

STEVE MARABOLI

DREAMING
IS JUST
THINKING WITH
YOUR HEART.

life isn't about
FINDING YOURSELF;
it's about
CREATING YOURSELF.

Anonymous

Keep
your eyes
on the stars
and your feet on the
ground.

THEODORE ROOSEVELT

THE ROAD TO HAPPINESS IS PAVED WITH RAINBOWS AND CUPCAKES.

SHOOT FOR THE MOON. EVEN IF YOU MISS, YOU'LL LAND AMONG THE STARS.

NORMAN VINCENT PEALE

FOLLOW YOUR DREAMS, WORK HARD, PRACTICE, AND PERSEVERE.

SASHA COHEN

YOU PROTECT YOUR
BEING WHEN YOU

love

YOURSELF BETTER.
THAT'S THE

secret.

ISABELLE ADJANI

MAKE YOUR WISHES AND

dreams

YOUR

reality.

I BELIEVE IN WRITING YOUR OWN STORY.

CHARLOTTE ERIKSSON

It's never

TOO LATE...

to be whoever you want

TO BE.

Eric Roth

SOMETIMES IT'S OK TO TOOT YOUR OWN HORN.

NO PESSIMIST EVER
DISCOVERED THE SECRETS
OF THE STARS, OR SAILED
TO AN UNCHARTED LAND,
OR OPENED A NEW DOORWAY
TO THE HUMAN SPIRIT.

HELEN KELLER

If you can **dream it,** you can **do it.**

TOM FITZGERALD

THE FINAL FORMING OF A PERSON'S CHARACTER LIES IN THEIR OWN HANDS.

ANNE FRANK

BE YOUR OWN
KIND OF
BEAUTIFUL.

WHAT WE DO FLOWS FROM WHO WE ARE.

PAUL VITALE

IT IS NOT WRONG TO BE DIFFERENT. SOMETIMES IT IS HARD, BUT IT IS NOT WRONG.

ELIZABETH MOON

FLY THROUGH

life

LIKE A RADIANT

Pegasus.

LOVE THE LIFE YOU LIVE, LIVE THE LIFE YOU LOVE.

BOB MARLEY

Laugh often,
DREAM BIG,
reach for the
STARS!

Anonymous

NOTHING EXCEPT THE IMPOSSIBLE SHALL OCCUR.

E. E. CUMMINGS

REACH HIGH,
FOR STARS LIE
HIDDEN IN YOUR
SOUL. DREAM
DEEP, FOR
EVERY DREAM
PRECEDES
THE GOAL.

PAMELA VAULL STARR

Hitch your wagon to a star.

RALPH WALDO EMERSON

I'M CRAZY, AND I DON'T PRETEND TO BE ANYTHING ELSE.

RIHANNA

YOU GET A BETTER

view

WITH YOUR HEAD IN THE

clouds.

WE ASK OURSELVES,
WHO AM I TO BE
BRILLIANT,
GORGEOUS,
HANDSOME,
TALENTED, AND
FABULOUS?
ACTUALLY, WHO ARE
YOU NOT TO BE?

MARIANNE WILLIAMSON

Your

SELF-WORTH

is defined by you. You don't have to depend on someone telling you

WHO YOU ARE.

Beyoncé

SHINE FROM THE

inside
out.

UNIQUENESS
IS WHAT MAKES
YOU BEAUTIFUL.

THERE IS NO CHANCE,
NO DESTINY, NO FATE
THAT CAN CIRCUMVENT
OR HINDER OR CONTROL
THE FIRM RESOLVE
OF A DETERMINED SOUL.

ELLA WHEELER WILCOX

IN DREAMS . . . THERE ARE NO IMPOSSIBILITIES.

JÁNOS ARANY

WE BECOME HAPPIER, MUCH HAPPIER, WHEN WE REALIZE LIFE IS AN OPPORTUNITY RATHER THAN AN OBLIGATION.

MARY AUGUSTINE

It is
not in the stars
to hold our
destiny but in
ourselves.

WILLIAM SHAKESPEARE

BE BRAVE ENOUGH TO LIVE CREATIVELY . . . WHAT YOU DISCOVER WILL BE WONDERFUL. WHAT YOU DISCOVER WILL BE YOURSELF.

ALAN ALDA

FIND THE
WONDER AND
MAGIC IN
EVERYTHING
YOU DO.

LET YOUR INNER UNICORN SHINE FOR ALL TO SEE.

I am

WHOEVER

★ I say I am. ★

America Ferrera

YOUR

greatest self

HAS BEEN WAITING YOUR

whole life;

DON'T MAKE IT WAIT ANY

longer.

STEVE MARABOLI

CHASE RAINBOWS EVERY SINGLE DAY.

JUST WHEN THE CATERPILLAR THOUGHT THE WORLD WAS ENDING, IT BECAME A BUTTERFLY.

ENGLISH PROVERB

BE IN LOVE
WITH YOUR LIFE,
EVERY DETAIL
OF IT.

JACK KEROUAC

RIDE THE

energy

OF YOUR OWN UNIQUE

spirit.

GABRIELLE ROTH

Seize
the day
and seize your
dreams.

WITHOUT LEAPS OF IMAGINATION, OR DREAMING, WE LOSE THE EXCITEMENT OF POSSIBILITIES.

GLORIA STEINEM

The most important kind of

FREEDOM

is to be what

YOU REALLY ARE.

Jim Morrison

THE FIRST STEP TO BEING MAGIC IS BELIEVING IN MAGIC.

IF YOU HAVE BUILT CASTLES
IN THE AIR, YOUR WORK NEED
NOT BE LOST; THAT IS WHERE
THEY SHOULD BE. NOW PUT
THE FOUNDATIONS
UNDER THEM.

HENRY DAVID THOREAU

YOU YOURSELF, AS MUCH AS

anybody

IN THE ENTIRE UNIVERSE,

deserve

YOUR LOVE AND AFFECTION.

ANONYMOUS

PUT YOUR EAR DOWN
CLOSE TO YOUR SOUL
AND LISTEN HARD.

ANNE SEXTON

NEVER LOSE SIGHT OF YOUR DREAMS.

IT TAKES COURAGE TO GROW UP AND BECOME WHO YOU REALLY ARE.

E. E. CUMMINGS

IF I AM NOT FOR MYSELF, WHO IS FOR ME?

HILLEL THE ELDER

love
the person
you were
born
to be.

TO BE YOURSELF IN
A WORLD THAT IS
CONSTANTLY TRYING TO
MAKE YOU SOMETHING
ELSE IS THE GREATEST
ACCOMPLISHMENT.

RALPH WALDO EMERSON

It's not selfish to
LOVE YOURSELF,
**take care of yourself, and
make your happiness a**
PRIORITY.
It's necessary.

Mandy Hale

YOU CAN BE THE RIPEST, JUICIEST PEACH IN THE WORLD, AND THERE'S STILL GOING TO BE SOMEBODY WHO HATES PEACHES.

DITA VON TEESE

BE
FIERCE
AND
FABULOUS.

KEEP SHINING,

beautiful one.

THE WORLD NEEDS YOUR

light.

ANONYMOUS

DO NOT FORGET YOUR DUTY TO LOVE YOURSELF.

SØREN KIERKEGAARD

OWN WHO

you
are.

PEOPLE
WANT TO PUT
YOU IN A BOX, BUT
I'M NOT A BOX. I'M
A HUMAN BEING.

TATIANA MASLANY

We should stop

DEFINING

**each other by what we are not,
and start defining ourselves**

by who we are.

Emma Watson

Owning your story is the **bravest** thing you will *ever do.*

BRENÉ BROWN

BE
MORE
UNICORN

WHOEVER IS HAPPY
WILL MAKE OTHERS
HAPPY TOO.

ANNE FRANK

INSTEAD OF LOOKING IN THE MIRROR AND FOCUSING ON YOUR FLAWS, LOOK IN THE MIRROR AND APPRECIATE YOUR BEST FEATURES . . . EVERYONE HAS THEM.

DEMI LOVATO

SPREAD YOUR SPARKLE EVERYWHERE.

SHINE, AND THE WHOLE

world

SHINES WITH

you.

FEET, WHAT DO I NEED YOU FOR WHEN I HAVE WINGS TO FLY?

FRIDA KAHLO

TO BE BEAUTIFUL
MEANS TO BE
YOURSELF. YOU
DON'T NEED TO BE
ACCEPTED BY OTHERS.
YOU NEED TO
ACCEPT
YOURSELF.

THÍCH NHẤT HẠNH

DREAMS
ARE THE
PLAYGROUNDS
OF UNICORNS.

I'm a big believer in accepting

YOURSELF

the way you are and not really worrying about it.

Jennifer Lawrence

Attitude is *everything.*

DIANE VON FÜRSTENBERG

I SAY IF I'M BEAUTIFUL.

I SAY IF I'M STRONG.

YOU WILL NOT

DETERMINE MY

STORY—I WILL.

AMY SCHUMER

MASTERING OTHERS IS STRENGTH. MASTERING YOURSELF IS TRUE POWER.

LAO TZU

IGNORE SELF-DOUBT AND INNER CONFLICT. DWELL ON POSITIVE THOUGHTS.

LAILAH GIFTY AKITA

NO ONE CAN MAKE YOU FEEL

inferior

WITHOUT YOUR

consent.

ELEANOR ROOSEVELT

TO DO:

shine,

sparkle,

AND HOLD YOUR HORN HIGH.

YOU HAVE TO BE UNIQUE AND DIFFERENT AND SHINE IN YOUR OWN WAY.

LADY GAGA

Image credits